1001 WAYS TO CALL-IN SICK

1001 WAYS TO CALL-IN SICK

or Take A Day Off From Work

TREEB

Copyright © 2008 by Treeb.

ISBN: Hardcover   978-1-4257-9123-0
             Softcover   978-1-4257-9114-8

All rights reserved. No part of this book may be reproduced or transmitted in any form or by any means, electronic or mechanical, including photocopying, recording, or by any information storage and retrieval system, without permission in writing from the copyright owner.

Disclosure:
This book is for entertainment purposes only. Any statements or facts listed are incidental. This book does not guarantee that you will not lose your job, put on probation, laid off, suspended, relocated, warning issued or any action associated with your employment/unemployment status.

This book was printed in the United States of America.

To order additional copies of this book, contact:
Xlibris Corporation
1-888-795-4274
www.Xlibris.com
Orders@Xlibris.com

42707

Dedication

To "YOU" who gave us instructions to "rest on the 7th day", I am eternally grateful that you dropped this in my spirit.

Book Summary:

A quick reference book filled with entertainment tips on how to take a day off to take care of yourself, family, friends, and pets or to do something that is important to you.

I'm tired, sick, ill, lazy, sleepy, drunk, angry, lost,

need help, tooth ache  , lost my way, co-workers driving me crazy,

stop breathing, terrorist threats, sunny day  , car accident,

gone fishing  , black mailed, child support, hate my boss

mental health day, confused, dog bite  , allergic reaction

suspended, harassed, road rage, semi-conscious, arrested, beat up

in the hospital  laid off, child support, court notice, flooding

snow day, broken leg, etc. etc . . . .

---

1. I need a mental health day.

2. My kid has the flu (sick).

3. I fell and hurt my back.

4. Contact a relative/friend who is in the medical profession and have him/her write you a doctor's note.

5. Pass a kidney stone while at work . . . . (everybody will know why you did not show up the next day).

6. My baby has the chicken pox.

7. It's February 29th. I only get paid for 365 days, not 366. (Leap year)

8. My husband has the chicken pox.

9. My brakes gave out on my car. I jumped out and injured my left side.

10. I'm feeling dizzy and can't drive.

11. My doctor called and he wants to see me in his office immediately!

12. I got a toothache.

13. I went to the dentist and my jaw aches.

14. The dentist performed surgery on me.

15. I went to the dentist and I am high on Novocain.

16. I went to the eye doctor and I can't see.

17. I believe I had a heart attack, so I'm going to stay in bed.

18. If your spouse is employed at the same job, have your wife/husband tell your boss that you are sick.

19. Upon your return from vacation call the office and tell them that you are sick from vacation and you need more time off.

20. Went on vacation and was food poisoned.

21. Call the office and tell them you are retiring. After a few days off, change your mind and go back to work.

22. I've fallen and can't get up.

23. My computer crashed and I hurt myself.

24. I went fishing and the hook got stuck in my mouth.

25. My dog died.

26. My kid has a fever.

27. My cat is sick.

28. A car hit my dog.

29. I was putting on my underwear and I threw out my back.

30. Something's wrong with me and I am not sure what it is!

31. I got a hangover.

32. I got caught in the rain and now I am sick.

33. I tripped and fell over a chair.

34. My allergies are making me sick.

35. I have a nosebleed.

36. I have a severe case of head lice.

37. My children have fleas.

38. I have hemorrhoids.

39. I have female problems.

40. I stomped my toe!

41. I have a sinus headache.

42. My car won't start.

43. I have a flat tire.

44. My hamster is sick and dying.

45. My girlfriend dumped me and I am heart broken (emotionally distraught).

46. I'm stressed!

47. I'm grieving over the death of my spouse (significant other).

48. My child is grieving.

49. I have a sore throat.

50. I have congiavitis (pink eye).

51. I went dancing all night and now I can't walk because of a sore hip.

52. I was in a car accident.

53. A car hit my kid.

54. I am having a medial check-up today.

55. My medication made me sick.

56. I broke out in hives from my medicine.

57. I took a cough, stuffy nose so you can sleep medicine for my cold. What I got was "no sleep".

58. I am honoring those who lost their life on September 11th.

59. I'm too tired from my other job.

60. I have poison ivy.

61. Dog bite.

62. Allergic reaction to a bee sting.

63. I'm waiting for my mother/father to die.

64. I have an earache.

65. Lost my glasses and I can't see.

66. The power went out in my neighborhood and I can't shit, shower or shave.

67. My car broke down on the way to work.

68. Schools out—snow day!

69. Hit in the face with a baseball.

70. Had a heat stroke.

71. Sunburned badly.

72. I don't feel motivated for bullshit today.

73. My husband requested that I stay home today to perform "wifely duties".

74. Bad hair day.

75. My feet are swollen.

76. My legs hurt.

77. Can't wear shoes because of my bunions.

78. I sampled foreign cuisine and it made me sick.

79. I am unable to stand because of varicose veins.

80. Having a senior moment-forgot it was a workday.

81. Received 2nd degree burns cooking on the grill.

82. Plumbing problems. The plumber is in route to my home.

83. My Alzheimer's mother/father is lost.

84. No baby sitter.

85. Where I work is making me sick.

86. My boss makes me sick.

87. My husband/wife just got called to active duty.

88. I got a fish bone stuck in my throat.

89. I stepped on a nail and injured my foot.

90. I had an allergic reaction to penicillin.
91. I'm feeling light headed.
92. Arthur (arthritis) is kicking my butt today!
93. I had a miscarriage.
94. I got beat up/jumped/assaulted.
95. I have a migraine headache.
96. My neighbor's dog kept me up all night with his howling.
97. I twisted my ankle.
98. I slipped and fell on ice.
99. I slipped, tripped and fell in the tub.
100. I fell down the steps.
101. My Prozac supply is depleted.
102. My best friend died last night.
103. I have been skunked!
104. I have birds in my house.
105. I was running and my breast hit my mouth and I bit my tongue.
106. I am coming down off a high of drugs and/or alcohol.
107. I partied all night long and I did not get any sleep.
108. I'm just tired. (Physical exhaustion)
109. My bones ached.

110. The perm took out all my hair.

111. Because I can!

112. I just hit the lottery. I need a day off to allow reality to set in.

113. I was struck by lightning!

114. I'm in a state of shock!

115. I'm in jail.

116. I'm depressed.

117. My job title requires that I take off so that I don't get sick.

118. My kid swallowed a tack.

119. I need to see my lawyer about my job trying to force me to retire.

120. There are bats in my house.

121. Kid(s) in the hospital.

122. I'm having an anxiety attack.

123. I can't talk.

124. A tree fell on me.

125. I ate too much candy and my tooth aches.

126. I believe I have Lyme's disease (note: you can really prolong this one).

127. I have bleeding gums.

128. Call your boss and tell him/her your plane has been hijacked.

129. Don't call-into work. Tell them you took some heavy medication and you didn't wake up until two days later.

130. I was hospitalized.

131. A wild animal attacked me.

132. I fainted on the way to work.

133. Someone broke into my house and robbed me.

134. My house is on fire!

135. My neighbor's house caught on fire and soot is in/on my house.

136. A tree fell on my house.

137. I am spiritually sick.

138. My child is missing.

139. I am having a carpal tunnel attack in my hands.

140. The police have charged me with inappropriate conduct in the men's bathroom at the mall.

141. I lost my contact and I cannot see.

142. My ex-wife came out of nowhere and dropped the kids at my doorstep this morning.

143. I am having blackouts.

144. Overeating made me sick.

145. I had minor surgery.

146. No more babies . . . . I getting a tubal legation (aka tubes tied).

147. I just had an abortion.

148. Someone slipped me a "Mickey".

149. My blood pressure was normal until I went to the doctors.

150. I just had a minor stroke.

151. My knees just gave out.

152. I'm overweight and I cannot walk.

153. My husbands/wife snoring kept me awake all night . . . I'm tired.

154. I worked so hard yesterday that I am too sore to work today.

155. I'm having bladder problems.

156. I have loose stools.

157. I lost my false teeth.

158. My legs are swollen.

159. My husband/wife assaulted me.

160. My child was abused.

161. My co-workers perfume is making me sick.

162. I have a crook in my neck and cannot move.

163. The doctors discovered a blood clot in my leg.

164. I injured myself exercising.

165. I went into diabetic shock.

166. I want to kill my bad ass kid(s) and the stress of this has made me sick.

167. I'm feeling suicidal.

168. I have time zone syndrome. (Jet lag)

169. I am allergic to hard work.

170. I have a steroid addiction.

171. The air condition broke in my house and it was so hot inside, I did not get any sleep.

172. I drank a bad batch of moonshine.

173. I'm lovesick.

174. My co-workers are harassing and stressing me out.

175. I bit into a sandwich and broke my tooth on a bone.

176. My bursitis is acting up in my shoulder.

177. I have ringworm on my hand, face, etc.

178. My husband (and or child) has been called to military duty.

179. The stitches from my surgery came apart.

180. I am a victim of identity theft and it's affecting my well-being.

181. Went to pick up my kids in another state and my car broke down.

182. Husband penis want go down!

183. Made love all night-can't walk today.

184. Freeze bite from cleaning windshield.

185. Kids didn't wake me in time-coffee maker would not work.

186. Car didn't turnover and neither did I!

187. My bigheaded kid was jumping on my bed while I was sleeping. He falls head first into my face. I have a black eye from my kid jumping on the bed.

188. Fell in tub—injured ankle.

189. Slipped on step-fell and hurt the back of my head.

190. I bumped my head on the bed while making love.

191. I got cheek burn from being pulled across the rug.

192. Nagging mother-n-law wont go home.

193. Mother-n-law cooked dinner! Need I say more?

194. Daughter brought home husband and kids to live with me.

195. My son or daughter wouldn't go to school.

196. My house alarm would not unlock-keyless entry exit.

197. I woke up and thought it was Sunday . . . . went back to bed.

198. It's a snow storm and I can't make it to work.

199. I had a fight with my wife.

200. The kitchen cabinet fell on top of me.

201. Someone threw a pencil and it struck me in the eye.

202. I have a knot on my head from the little lady next door hitting me with her cane.

203. I have been sexually assaulted.

204. I'm sick from "fasting".

205. I lost my hair (It was in the bag when I bought it from the store).

206. I'm feigning for my girl (can't think).

207. I believe I have been in contact with Anthrax.

208. I am seeking medical attention and a Lawyer. I just discovered the government placed toxic chemicals and medicines in the water supply.

209. Bit by a mosquito while traveling. I may have West Nile Virus.

210. I was attacked by a swarm of bees.

211. I'm brain dead today.

212. I have a reoccurrence pain from a previous injury to my shoulder.

213. Muscle strain from walking and carrying heavy load.

214. Struck knee on a metal latch protruding from side of a container.

215. Descending wet steps, fell and bruised tailbone.

216. I overhead my boss talking negatively about me. I am emotionally stressed.

217. A letter flew into the air and struck me in my eye.

218. I misjudge the weight distribution of something I had piled up and it toppled and hit me in the head.

219. It's my birthday!

220. I blacked out! What day is it?

221. Deer crashed into the side of my car.

222. Huge tree fell on my car.

223. Foreign object flew into my eye-causing irritation.

224. Felt tightness in my chest while driving.

225. I had my son start my car and he accidentally put the car in reverse and smashed a hole in my garage.

226. I slipped on mud-injured right wrist.

227. I have difficulty moving my legs because of a pre-existing back injury.

228. Accidentally closed car door on fingers.

229. I slipped and banged my face on the car mirror.

230. Stepped into truck, slipped and fell striking my chest against the steering wheel.

231. If your manager is a sports fan, let him know that you have basketball tickets to see (name the #1 sports figure) play.

232. Stepped down from ladder, caught lower back and tailbone on a mechanic's tool box.

233. Attempted to change light bulb without proper eye protection. The bulb broke and glass is lodged in my eye.

234. I have numbness in my legs.

235. While cleaning my gun, I accidentally shot myself in the foot.

236. I was arrested for DWB (Driving While Black).

237. My neighbor assaulted me.

238. I am a witness to _____.
    (fill in the blank)

239. The IRS is auditing me.

240. Frostbite to foot and toes.

241. Stress due to my pending commute to work.

242. Racial profiling on the rise.

243. I can't decide whether I'm a girl or a boy today.

244. A Peeping Tom violated me.

245. I'm rich and I don't have to work!

246. I'm snowed in.

247. Injured while shoveling snow.

248. Call off sick with **Montezuma's** Revenge. If someone asked what it is, start gurgling into the phone, scream and hang up.

249. I have the flu.

250. Cite the 24-hour fever when you return to work just one day after calling off.

251. Pour spoiled milk on your shirt, go to work and tell your colleagues you don't feel well today—you yakked before coming to work . . . watch people flee.

252. I gave blood donation and had some complications while donating. They can't stop my bleeding.

253. I was attacked by a rabid dog in route to my car.

254. Ed McMann, Dick Clark just sent you an envelope that clearly states "you are to remain at home to receive your million dollar check" . . . . today!

255. Weed your garden and deliberately touch poison ivy, poison sumac with your bare hands. Then touch various parts of your body or go to work and touch others.

256. Call your boss and alert him/her that the "deer tick bite" that you thought you has was actually diagnosed by the doctor as the worst case of genital crabs he has ever seen. Offer to show this to the boss and as he/she declines, scream into the phone and hang up.

257. Fell on ice and hit head on ground.

258. Shoveling snow when my feet slipped out from under me, causing me to fall on shovel injuring elbow and side.

259. I have more education, responsibilities and years of service than my co-workers and they earn more money than I do.

260. I have the symptoms of a Stroke.

261. Truck slid into my parked car-damage to vehicle.

262. Struck in the head by broken glass from 2nd floor building.

263. Existing Reynard's Syndrome caused by environmental conditions aggravated by cold temperatures.

264. Elevated blood pressure due to personal incident.

265. Dumping garbage-experience extreme pain in groin area.

266. While jogging, I sprained hip.

267. Police pulled me over and I ran into his fist.

268. Abused by Police.

269. A large balloon float fell on me at the parade.

270. Go to work and pretend you have diarrhea-run back and forth to the bathroom the first ½ hour of the day.

271. I discovered the woman I married used to be a man.

272. If you're ugly-don't wear make-up. Everyone will swear you are sick and tell you to go home.

273. Pretend that your medication is giving you mood swings . . . have outburst, mood swings for ½ hour.

274. State your husband was injured and you are the only person who can take care of him.

275. Your husband is away on business and you have not heard from him in days. You're going to hop on a plane to see about him.

276. I slipped in a water puddle in the store, twice. I fell entering and exiting store.

277. I got menstrual cramps.

278. Stepped off bus and was hit by a car.

279. I broke my neck.

280. I was laughing so hard . . . I urinated on myself.

281. Had a flu shot. My arm is sore.

282. Pretzel got caught in my throat.

283. Running up the steps naked, I missed a step and injured every body part that had never seen the sun.

284. My father punched me in the eye.

285. Broke my collarbone playing football.

286. I accidentally closed the door on my hand.

287. I accidentally locked my baby in the car while it's running . . . my nerves are bad.

288. I need a change of perspective.

289. I'm working on myself and I need the day off.

290. Removing rubber bands from bundles of mail, when a rubber band broke and hit me in the eye.

291. Car ran red light and struck my vehicle at the intersection.

292. Forklift ran over my foot.

293. I'm a secret agent and my cover has been blown. I will call you in a few days when I have a new identity.

294. My husband just called and stated "he is leaving me" after _____ years of marriage. I need time to find him. (fill in blank #)

295. I ran a marathon and I have blisters on my feet.

296. Wearing high heel boots, my heel broke and I broke my foot.

297. Say you were abducted by aliens and you just return to earth too tired to work.

298. I worked two hours comp time for four days straight. I am taking the day off (eight hours).

299. I was locked in a bank vault overnight. I just got out today.

300. Went camping in the mountains and got lost.

301. I was ran over by a reindeer.

302. I am experiencing blurring.

303. I lost my money in Atlantic City and I got to find it.

304. I see dead people at work!

305. My ears are ringing.

306. The movers lost all of my belongings (furniture, clothes, etc.) relocating to a new state.

307. I caught my best friend having sex with my husband/wife.

308. I was busted soliciting a hooker and using the company money to pay for the services.

309. I have blisters in my mouth.

310. My hair caught on fire.

311. My cancer medicine is making me sick.

312. I had a conversation with myself and we decided to stay home.

313. Someone stole my mink coat and I am sick over it.

314. The wild meat I ate was too wild.

315. Brain freeze!

316. I have an irregular heartbeat.

317. I saw my life flash in front of me . . . . dead end job!

318. I'm in a state of panic!

319. I'm shell shock from the war.

320. When I awaken, I did not feel like me.

321. I've gain so much weight that I can't get out of bed.

322. I'm having erotica thoughts about my boss and I can't effectively work with him/her.

323. I forgot where my job is located.

324. I realize I work for Enron.

325. One of those days where compost happens.

326. No one will notice I'm not their.

327. When opportunity knocks to do something else, I must surrender.

328. There is water over bridge. There is no other throughway to work.

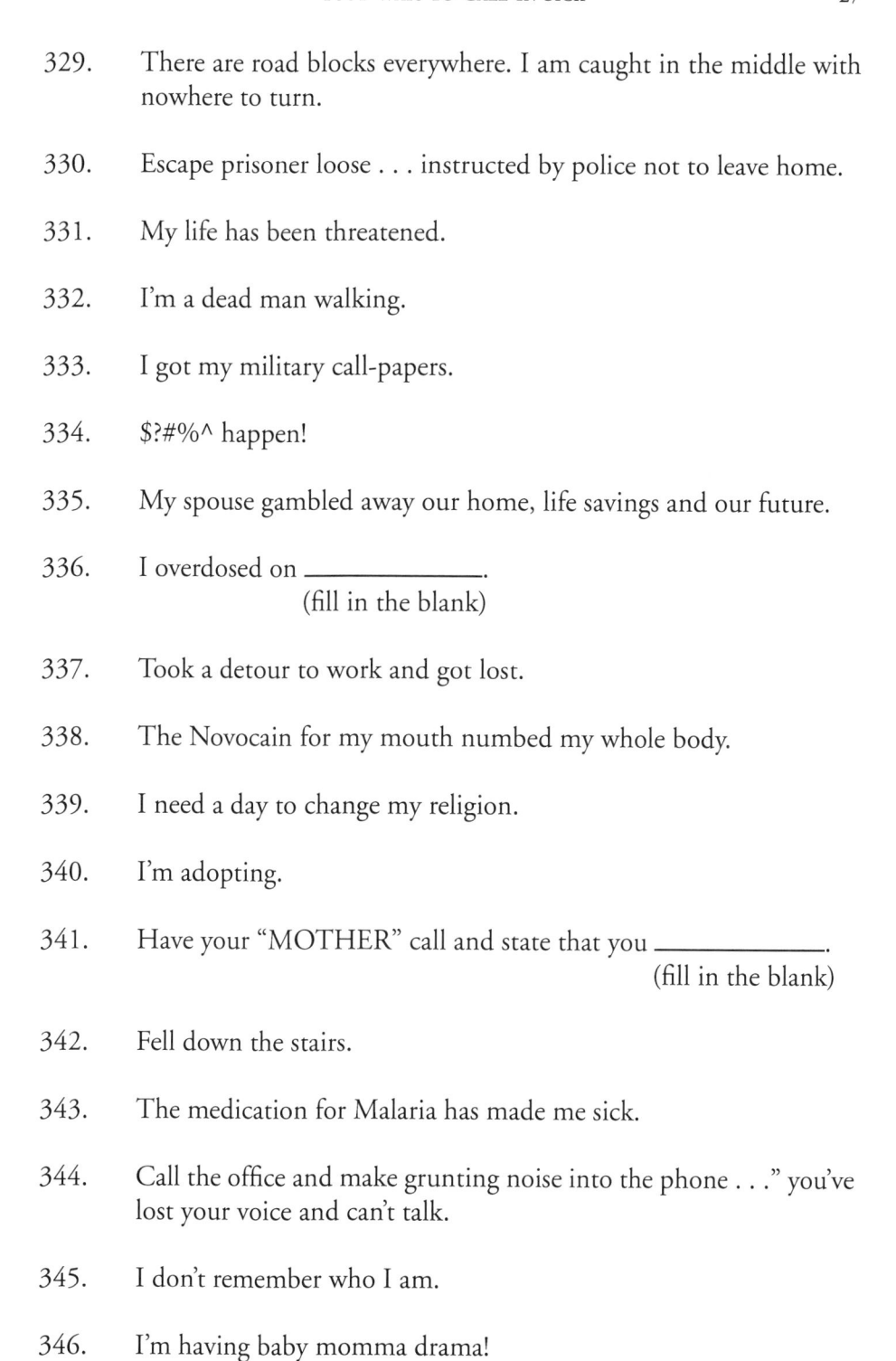

329. There are road blocks everywhere. I am caught in the middle with nowhere to turn.

330. Escape prisoner loose . . . instructed by police not to leave home.

331. My life has been threatened.

332. I'm a dead man walking.

333. I got my military call-papers.

334. $?#%^ happen!

335. My spouse gambled away our home, life savings and our future.

336. I overdosed on _____.
(fill in the blank)

337. Took a detour to work and got lost.

338. The Novocain for my mouth numbed my whole body.

339. I need a day to change my religion.

340. I'm adopting.

341. Have your "MOTHER" call and state that you _____.
(fill in the blank)

342. Fell down the stairs.

343. The medication for Malaria has made me sick.

344. Call the office and make grunting noise into the phone . . ." you've lost your voice and can't talk.

345. I don't remember who I am.

346. I'm having baby momma drama!

347. I'm lethargic!

348. I've lowered my cholesterol.

349. I am too fat for the TV camera. The job gave me one (1) week to drop the weight.

350. My car caught on fire.

351. I don't want to be around people who don't believe what I believe.

352. I came ready to work, but there was "no work".

353. Someone ran me off the road. I'm all shook up.

354. I'm doing a 21-day consecration from work.

355. I'm caught up in the spirit (religious, spiritual, earth, etc.).

356. I called in and (insert name) answered the phone. Too bad you did not get the message.

357. My grandmother is dying and I need the day off. (this works good the day before or after a holiday).

358. I'm tired of everyone blaming me for everything gone wrong. I'm off today.

359. While changing a light fixture, I smelled burnt flesh . . . . I need some time off.

360. I walked under a ladder . . . . . 30 days bad luck.

361. I received a chain letter to stay away from work a few days or I will have bad luck. (send a copy of your letter to your boss)

362. My drug addicted husband stole my car and keys.

363. The sheriff confiscated my home and car.

364. The holidays have come and gone. I'm feeling depressed.

365. Someone stole all my clothes.

366. My pierce tongue is infected.

367. I went rollerblading with my kids and fell, hurting my hip, leg, back and ankle.

368. My allergies are so bad, I can't see to drive.

369. I opened the newspaper, read the obituary, saw my name listed and got sick to my stomach.

370. Fifteen women at work . . . . one bathroom. You do the math!

371. I gave a friend a ride to the store and unbeknownst to me, he robbed the store. I drove away and I'm in police custody for armed robbery.

372. My babysitter quit on me today.

373. Piss your boss off really bad and call out sick the next day with stress.

374. Have the clergy call your job with bad news.

375. Have a family call several times to your job. You start to cry and jump up grab your coat and leave running, yelling . . ." I can't believe it! I can't believe it!

376. Pretend to have a heart attack at work.

377. Talk about your dead love one or animal. Become hysterical with tears.

378. My kid got on the wrong school bus this morning. We are still looking for him.

379. Go to work. Say that the smell of (fill in the blank) makes you sick. Go home ill.

380. Sleep in your work clothes. Don't shower, brush teeth . . . tell everyone that you did not have time to go home and change for the past two days.

381. I had a sex change and need time to adjust to the new me.

382. "Pass gas" while at work. Do it as much as possible. People will get sick of it and tell you to go home.

383. Go to the doctors and complain that something is wrong with you. Get a note for a few days off.

384. My job picked me to go to Iraq and I need a few days to digest the news.

385. I slept on the couch all week and now my neck, back, legs are numb.

386. I went skiing and froze my balls off.

387. In my country it is customary to take off once a month to rejuvenate the mind.

388. If I don't use it . . . . I lose it.

389. Go to work horny as hell. Grab a magazine, find a secluded spot and relieve yourself. Make sure that your boss knows where you are at so he/se can find you.

390. My father just had a stroke and is being rushed to the hospital as we speak.

391. My father is having surgery. My mother needs to be put in a nursing home. My wife is threatening to leave me. My son attempted suicide and my daughter ran away from home.

392. Paper cut caused excessive bleeding.

393. Call your job and state that after all the surgeries you had for liposuction, tummy tuck, face lift, ass left, you are not feeling like yourself. You are in pain.

394. Frostbite!

395. I burnt my tongue while cooking.

396. Deliberately run into a door and claim you got punched in the eye.

397. Stand outside while it is lightning and claim you where struck with after currents from an actual lightning strike MANY yards away.

398. Bang your head several times against a wall and tell your boss you where jumped by an unknown group of people.

399. You where abducted by aliens.

400. Your husband just got out of jail and you need time off to get him adjusted to society.

401. Your husband/wife is home from military (war) and you need family (re-acquainted) time.

402. You have no will or desire to work.

403. I drank contaminated water.

404. My boss humiliated me in front of my coworkers.

405. Take a walk through the woods where you know there are ticks. Call your job and say you have Lyme disease.

406. "Hot" coffee was spilled in my lap.

407. It's a bad snow day. Attempt to drive to work. Call-in and say you are stuck on the roadway, unable to come in. (oh yeah, make sure you are near a mall when you break down).

408. Idling car in "closed" garage you felt dizzy and sick.

409. Start a commuting club and it's the other person turn to drive. You have no other means of transportation. The driver never shows up.

410. Your driveway is on a slope. It's very icy and you can't drive up the slope to exit.

411. Hit a huge pothole. Call-in and state that your car is smoking.

412. Call-in and say you have four (4) flat tires.

413. Claim an illness and every once in a while, have it flare up.

414. The medication I'm on has given me hemorrhoids.

415. I got punched in the eye with my glasses on.

416. Know your boss. Find out he/she weakness and use it. (E.g. If your boss has a weakness for sick kids, use the sick kid excuse or if your boss grew up around females, use the "I have female problems" excuse).

417. Cut yourself shaving, don't stop the blood and go to work.

418. Create a history or as the saying goes "shit happens!" You fall and break your arm on ice, next year you are in a terrible car accident in icy conditions. Now, every year there is an ice storm, call out. You have become neurotic and paranoid during this time of year.

419. According to DMV I still have outstanding violations that need to be addressed immediately.

420. There is a nasty rumor circulating about me at work concerning the "Mall" bathroom with someone of the same sex. My picture is posted everywhere. I am embarrassed. It wasn't me!

421. I got lockjaw from the deliveryman.

422. Is it a workday?

423. I heard the company is downsizing so I'm doing you a favor and taking the day off.

424. Alcohol relapse-Binge.

425. I've been bleeding for 12 days or more.

426. I'm having heart palpitations from drinking too many cups of coffee.

427. Claim somebody shot at you on the way to work and now you are a nervous wreck.

428. On your way to work someone threw a brick from the bridge and broke your windshield and you are on your way to the hospital.

429. I'm shell-shocked!

430. Too much snow/ice on the road unable to drive far, but I made it to the (mall, diner, movie theater, etc.)

431. Snake bite.

432. I just received shocking news.

433. I stepped on a needle/nail.

434. My mom is dying of cancer. I want to be with her.

435. I have a bad case of bad breath.

436. I'm reaping what I sow.

437. The end does not justify the means.

438. I need time to conceal my sin.

439. I'm trying to avoid the ridiculous.

440. I'm the architect of my own life today.

441. Hot grits were thrown in my face.

442. I looked in the mirror and I don't like what I see.

443. Your favorite Manager had a heart attack and died. You were very close to him/her.

444. Join an organization where golf, fishing, surfing and power naps are part of the company business plan.

445. I have short people stigma.

446. When the numbers are up, I'm up. When the numbers are down, I'm down. This perpetual living is discouraging and detrimental to my well-being.

447. I talked myself sick.

448. I'm getting married.

449. I stayed up all night watching the Grammy's.

450. I have shingles.

451. I attempted suicide and failed.

452. I started a new job.

453. Call-in and say "I'm working like I don't need the money".

454. It's my holiday
Ben Franklin's Birthday Day
Ground Hog Day
International Working Women's Day
April Fools Day
National World Health Day
Earth Day
V-E day (Victory in Europe Day)
"D" Day
National Parents Day
Mother-in-Law Day

455. My mode of transportation is broken.

456. You are in a major department store trying on clothing in the dressing room and you hear laughter from the other side of the mirrored wall.

457. Go visit your love one at the graveyard—call your job and say your loved one told you "that you are working too hard"—take the day off.

458. Go to work and have crying fits. This should get you a couple of days off.

459. Plan your wedding during the week. The day of the wedding—get cold feet and run away. Call-in with the "wedding blues".

460. A serial killer is stalking me. I'm afraid to go outside.

461. My wife and girlfriend are sick. I must take care one or the other.

462. I'm taking a day off to off-set my retirement.

463. Eat something at the office party that makes you sick. Call out the next day.

464. In my dream it is the weekend . . . when I awaken, it's a workday.

465. The J—O—B is
        K
      I
     L
    L
   I
  N
 G
ME!

466. I was stuck in an elevator.

467. I am suffering from BOGO.

468. I stepped in a hole and was attacked by bees.

469. I'm being sexually harassed by a (you decide which gender).

470. Travel long distance from home. State that you gave your kid the keys to open the car and the kid accidentally locked them in the truck along with your pocketbook, ID, money, etc. Make sure this happens on a Sunday. (This will get you at least two days off.)

471. I'm snowed in.

472. Someone put a "Jinx" on me.

473. I awaken with rotten teeth and foul breath.

474. I have a lump growing out the back of my neck causing me pain.

475. I have been told to "Go "F" yourself" so many times that I have decided to act on it.

476. Recovering from surgery (<u>enter type of surgery</u>).

477. Donated blood . . . . now I need it for surgery.

478. Donated blood and now I feel faint.

479. Go hang out with a bunch of snotty nose kids—you're guaranteed to pick up something to make you sick.

480. If you're over 40—work on your "honey do list" all day long . . . . you won't be able to move the next day.

481. I got fired from my other job and I am not taking it well.

482. Go to work talking on a cordless phone (the kind you hook up in your house). People will think you're crazy.

483. Your husband is overseas at war—have depression episodes (real or unreal).

484. You were injured in a car accident on Monday, fixed car on Tuesday, someone hit your car again on Wednesday, fix car on Thursday and while it was parked on Friday . . . . it was hit again.

485. I am 70 years old and just discovered that my (wife/woman/girlfriend) is having a baby.

486. I just left (separated/divorce) my spouse and we work at the same job. I'm afraid of him/her.

487. I don't have to work. My husband is rich.

488. I have blended family issues.

489. Become a religious lunatic and people will avoid working with you.

490. The player just got played.

491. One eye starts to twitch un-controllably when you enter the Job (lobby) or when your boss name is uttered.

492. Bring your cat to work and claim you can't separate yourself from your twin.

493. For the 3rd time you're passed up for a promotion and don't know about it until someone else in the office informs you. (Now is the time to throw a fit, kick a chair or start talking and answering your self)

494. You called your mother for career counseling and she tells you to take the day off.

495. Call—in a bomb scare.

496. Bring your shrink to work with you.

497. While driving my steering wheel became unlocked. So I was unable to drive.

498. Involved in car accident-injured elbow entire arm swollen.

499. Too much pollen in air-eyes swollen, sneezing, can't breath.

500. Throw a huge party (100+) invite co-workers (everybody know you throw the best parties) so when you call-out the next day nobody will notice you missing.

501. Kill off the whole family. Tell them:
1st excuse: Mother was shot
2nd excuse: Kid was raped and kidnapped
3rd excuse: Son hanged his self
4th excuse: wife died from childbirth

502. Become a habitual liar. No one will ever believe anything you say.

503. Boating accident—injured family members.

504. A shark attacked me.

505. I fell asleep on the beach and never woke up.

506. I was buried in the sand up to my neck and could not get out.

507. You have two wooden prosthesis . . . call in and say you broke your ankle.

508. I ate everything at the "all you can eat" buffet today. I'm sick.

509. Deliberately eat raw meat that has been sitting out . . . this will get you a few days, weeks, months . . . maybe check out forever.

510. Drive through the worse part of town to order "take-out food". Your goal is to get car jacked, held up or something.

511. Sit on a packet of tomato ketchup and everyone will think you're bleeding.

512. Sit on mustard-have some run down your leg. People will think you have (fill in the blank) on yourself.

513. Do everything for your boss, get coffee, buy his lunch, hang up his coat, run errands, sleep with him, but . . . don't get attached to him/her emotionally. When the time comes and you need a day off-get very emotional about everything-telling all the co-workers how good you have been to him/her.

514. In the middle of a meeting-have someone call you several times. You must leave because it's a family emergency.

515. Be a busy body and noisy in everyone's business. Your co-workers would hate to see you coming and will be glad to see you take a day off.

516. I found a lump in my breast.

517. The gossip on the job is killing me.

518. Come hell or high water, I need some time off to take care of me.

519. I don't have the tenacity to go to work.

520. The "enemy" is attacking me!

521. My face is "jacked up" because of disastrous facial.

522. I got involved in **OPP** and I'm **MIA**, because the **MOB** wants me to **RIP**.

523. I'm a witness to a crime and I'm in protective custody.

524. I ran away and can't find my way back.

525. I have "road work rage".

526. I went to an air balloon show and today I can't look down.

527. I'm shell shock-post trauma.

528. No pay-no work! (The company did not pay you for work performed).

529. Walking with umbrella in hand I was struck by lightning.

530. I caught my spouse cheating and I'm in shock!

531. The next day I kill the bitch!

532. Bit by a snake.

533. While exercising I hurt my _____.
(fill in the blank)

534. I'm wounded and bleeding all over the land.

535. My kid is away at camp and is homesick. You must drive to pick him/her up immediately because he is threatening to run away.

536. Need family time.

537. Put calamine lotion (the pink stuff) all over you hands, neck, face etc. Go to work you are surely to be sent home.

538. Shot 50 times by the police.

539. Working with chemicals, I accidentally touched my eye (hospital here I come).

540. Took my kid to the amusement park and his finger was caught between a harness bar on the ride (cut finger).

541. I went to Las Vegas . . . lost my soul and now I'm sick to death.

542. I have a boil/cyst between my buttocks and I must have it removed surgically.

543. My family thought I was dead and buried me alive.

544. I'm feeling crazy and deranged.

545. At a meeting you don't want to be at, have some one call your cell phone and say _____.
(fill in the blank)

546. Find a good doctor and have him/her diagnosis you with various ailments. Anytime you need a day off, use one of them.

547. My house was robbed.

548. As a bus driver, say that the school children are always threatening to beat you up and now you are traumatized.

549. You commute via the train everyday to work. State that you are being stalked by another passenger.

550. I'm addicted to "Oprah". Showtime's 9:00, 10, 1:00 pm, 6:00, 7, etc.

551. I have a hang nail.

552. I've lost the "pep" in my step.

553. "Be I whole" is half.

554. I am buying a new car and I had to turn my old car into trade.

555. I'm thinking of a lie.

556. I'm not gay, lesbian, transgender, bi-sexual. I'm just confused.

557. I'm not White, Black, Chinese, Indian or Spanish. I just confused.

558. I'm getting a new boss and the thought of it is making me sick.

559. You are eligible to retire, so you go to the doctors and get a note stating you need time off for any illness that has a long name.

560. I'm going blind.

561. At lunch time, sit in your parked car with sunglasses on and point a hair dryer at passing cars . . . . need I say more.

562. Every time someone asks you to do something, ask if they want fries with that.

563. Finish all your sentences with "in accordance with the prophecy".

564. Put mosquito netting around your work area and play tropical sound all day.

565. I'm moving.

566. No heat in the house.

567. I went under the knife and the surgery went bad.

568. According to my zodiac reading, I need the day off to _____.
(fill in the blank)

569. I'm a Marrow donor today.

570. Too many terror alerts. I'm afraid to leave my home.

571. In my imagination I am sick . . . . so be it!

572. Casting for a role, someone stated "break-a-leg" and I broke a leg.

573. I had a heart attack while shoveling snow.

574. Airplane crashed into my car.

575. The barber cut my head with dirty clippers and I have huge bumps all over my head.

576. Working at the pizzeria and burned my arm.

577. As a barmaid I got caught between a bar fight.

578. I divorced my (fill in the blank) and now I'm going through the seven steps of withdrawal.

579. I'm allergic to telephones, cell phones, fax machines and copiers.

580. When you turn the air off or close all the windows at work, I can't breath.

581. As a police officer, I attempted to retrieve my gun from the holster and I shot myself.

582. I contacted the sexually transmitted disease called Sleeper Sex.

    (See you when I wake up).

583. Shopping in the hardware store, a box fell from the top shelf and hit me in the head.

584. I'm stuck on a "kiddy" ride.

585. I woke up with a pain in my ass . . . . it was my husband (wife).

586. Transported to hospital because I got cut by the barbers straight razor.

587. In the midst of a hurricane, I lost everything.

588. I got stuck in a Poker Tournament.

589. Someone siphon all of my gasoline out of my car.

590. I passed out at the nail salon.

591. Hung Lo calls work and says, "Hey, boss I no come work today. I really sick. I got headache, stomach ache and my legs hurt. I no come work." The boss says, "You know Hung Lo, I really need you today. When I feel like that, I go to my wife and tell her give me sex. That makes everything better and I go work. You try that." Two hours

later Hung Lo calls again. "Boss, I do what you say and I feel great. I be at work soon. You got nice house."

592. I'm stuck on a cruise ship.

593. A woman calls her boss one morning and tells him that she is staying home because she is not feeling well. "What the matter? He asks. "I have a case of anal glaucoma? I can't see my ass coming into work today.

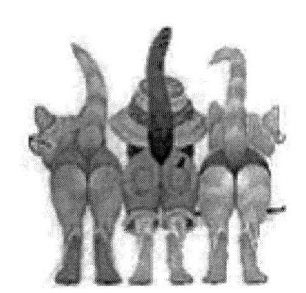

594. I've fallen and I can't get up.

595. I am involved in gang related activities.

596. I was shot out of a canon and missed my target.

597. The union/employees blocking the entrance to the work place.

598. Call and state that you are afraid "terrorist" may bomb your building.

599. I was caught in an avalanche.

600. Your friend is seriously ill. Call-in and say that you are going to spend sometime at the hospital with him/her.

601. When your company has a fire drill, leave and don't return after it is over. Say that you were told to "leave" the building. So you went home.

602. The costume you were wearing at the company's Halloween Party frighten you . . . now you are traumatized and going out on stress.

603. At the company annual party, talk bad about your boss; complain about his management style or what he/she wears. The next day call out sick from an alcohol or drug hangover.

604. You commute via a train and it passes your stop every day.

605. Plan to attend off-site meeting. Have someone else sign you in and take your place. This works really well if you are traveling out of state and no one knows your identity.

606. It's Martin Luther King Birthday. You are traumatized by the fact that it is not a National Holiday.

607. Come to work and act like you're the boss. Make sure you tell your boss what to do. (I suspect they will recommend bed rest)

608. (If you need **Wednesday** off.) Go to work on Monday, fake injury on Tuesday, etc. etc.

609. Go to a meeting off-site that does not exist.

610. Sleep with the timekeeper. You will be covered for any absences. (should I say more?)

611. Step in front of a moving bus (but don't let the bus hit you). Now you are traumatized.

612. Call-in and state you just experienced the worse case of road rage when you accidentally cut someone off and they followed you until you came to a stop. The person got out of their vehicle, walked up to you and proceeds to punch at you through closed windows. The person was kicking the car, spitting, etc.

613. While the equipment is moving at work, jump to get out of the way before you are hurt. State that this frightens you and you need time off to "get your bearings".

614. Puddle of water in front of store/mall entrance. You accidentally fall in lobby. Not enough to break a bone but enough to get you a few days off.

615. Communicate all day long that you killed somebody. Before you know it, management will be sending you home for bed rest (or to jail).

616. Have an allergic reaction at work.

617. I was jacking off and injured my penis.

618. I am having involuntary vaginal muscle spasms. I must seek therapy to stop it.

619. I have a sex addition . . . . seeking therapy.

620. I saw mommy kissing Santa Claus, so I shot him.

621. Aliens kidnapped me.

622. WORK. I tried it, didn't like it . . . . I'm going home.

623. Yell, scream, and get overly excited during a sports game with your boss. (football, basket ball, hockey, etc.) Scream out "You play like my bosses mother!"

624. As my wife was driving the truck, the tire blew. Her reflective back hand to protect me, knocked me unconscious.

625. Share your homemade wine with everyone at work, you don't drink any. Leave work with everyone feeling spirited.

626. I'm stuck in a crawl space.

627. I'm locked/hiding in a closet in another man's house.

628. I am a "runaway bride or groom".

629. Put your face on a milk carton in the employee's refrigerator with the saying "Missing-have you seen this person?"

630. Chased or attacked by a bear, stuck in a tree.

631. Had a party with the KKK.... "I'm a little tied up"

632. While roller bladding/skating, I fell and broke my _____.
(fill in the blank)

633. A hockey puck hit me square in the face.

634. I called out sick, went to the baseball game, they showed my picture on TV and now I'm really sick!

635. Call out UGLY.

636. My head is stuck in the head rail.

637. Stuck on a broke down bus in the middle of no-where.

638. I saw the movie "Rosewood" and now I am too angry (pissed off) to work around Caucasian people.

639. Ingrown toe nail.

640. I am allergic to people at work.

641. Frying chicken. I did not realize grease was on floor, slipped hit pan, hot grease all over me.

642. Struck by lightning.

643. Truck dislodge and rammed into my house, car, building.

644. I didn't get the "message" that I was to report to work today.

645. I have all the time in the world to work.

646. I was lost in an avalanche.

647. I had a reality check with my child-and now I need a day off to re-group

648. It's the only day available for me to _____.
     (fill in the blank)

649. I take this day off every year.

650. Hit in the face with a snowball . . . . you should see my face.

651. **(Company Policy)** . . . Use it or lose it!

652. The Government made me do it.

653. I'm on my way to Washington DC to see the President.

654. My dog ate the electrical cord . . . well you can guess the rest.

655. Fell asleep and woke up a different person.

656. My wife meatloaf has staying power.

657. Male: I'm getting in touch with my feminine side

658. Female: I'm getting in touch with my manly side.

659. Caught in a mudslide.

660. It's raining outside. Haven't you heard? "Brown sugar don't get wet!'

661. Work makes me sick.

662. Pretend that you don't know how to do something (use it on a lot of things) other people will do your work because they feel "you can't do anything"(so you won't be missed if you take a day off)

663. You are juggling "moral issue" and "bad employee" issue at work. Take the day off.

664. Company has to find ways to spend/save money, so they encourage you to take a day off.

665. Dislocated shoulder while playing with grand children.

666. The cat unplugged the alarm clock.

667. I have the "Entitlement" mentality.

668. I have to go to my mother's dog funeral (He *was* family).

669. I have the swine flu.

670. I forgot the way to work.

671. I was arrested because of mistaken identity.

672. I work with a group of people that have just been released from jail. I'm afraid to turn my back or bend over.

673. I tripped over my dog and was knocked unconscious.

674. My bus broke down and was held up by robbers.

675. I forgot to come back to work after lunch.

676. I couldn't find my shoes.

677. I hurt myself bowling.

678. I was spit on by a venomous snake.

679. I totaled my wife's car in a collision with a cow (deer, horse, etc.).

680. A "hit man" is looking for me at work.

681. My curlers burned my hair and I had to go to the hairdresser.

682. I eloped!

683. My brain went to sleep and I couldn't wake up.

684. I had to be there for my husband grand jury trial.

685. I had to ship my grandmothers bones to India.

686. I forgot what day of the week it is . . . . I thought it was my day off.

687. I need time off to settle my mother/father estate.

688. My monkey died.

689. Need time to attend to personal errand(s).

690. Catching up on sleep.

691. Simply relaxing.

692. Attend my kid school event.

693. I buried my money and I must find it.

694. The train service shut down.

695. I'm waiting on God for instruction.

696. I work here!?

697. I have so many jobs that I thought this one gave me the day off!

698. I'm celebrating my job anniversary.

699. I set the clock one hour ahead so I wouldn't be late. My wife set it one hour back so she would not over sleep and my dog just slept on the damn thing.

700. I'm providing a momentary distraction from life's tedium.

701. Talking in my sleep kept me up all night.

702. Eat seven day old greens. (need I say more?)

703. Have a out of body experience at work (rant & rave in a séance mode).

704. Fall in a pile of sh??t and go to work. Act like nothing is wrong.

705. Tell your boss that you're taking anger management classes.

706. Every job has a few penalties.

707. Truck windows and locks are frozen shut.

708. A tornado was headed towards me. I started running, I jumped, I screamed. I awaken myself out of a dream. I bumped my head on the dresser, causing a gash in my head.

709. Go to work on Monday and realize that you forgot how to do your job.

710. I have agoraphobia (fear of open spaces) and can't work in this small cubicle.

711. My hero was assassinated.

712. A great leader died and out of respect, I'm taking the day off.

713. Six people where just killed on the job. I'm afraid I might be number seven.

714. If I go to work, I will be fired.

715. I'm stuck on a roller coaster.

716. I'm sitting on top of my car in the middle of a water/river flood, awaiting for emergency assistance.

717. My job is down sizing. I need the day off to find another job.

718. Day after the Super Bowl, and my team won!

719. I'm serving my country.

720. At Mickey D's buying coffee when some jerk comes in, robs the place and shoot the server.

721. Riding bike home and was hit by motorist.

722. Stuck in a snow blizzard in a broke down ambulance.

723. Attacked by squirrels.

724. I delivered my own child.

725. I had a vision/intuition that something bad was going to happen at work today

726. I'm superstitious. It's Friday the 13th!

727. Working with inferior products will ruin my reputation for proving quality to my customers.

728. I can't find my green card!

729. Immigration after me.

730. I owe the boss money.

731. I'm getting fired, laid off, down sized tomorrow. So why should I come in today?

732. I'm being stalked and the stalker knows where I work.

733. I received 24 boxes of condoms and I'm trying to use them all!

734. Make a trail of tomato juice on the floor leading to the rest rooms. Let someone find you in there gurgitating in the toilet.

735. When your boss asks you if you finished that project, begin to cry and ask "why can't you people just leave me alone"?

736. Go into the coffee room, shut the door and wait a while. After a few minutes, start yelling "there is no toilet paper in here"!

737. Call-in sick to the person you know called out sick the same day and leave a message.

738. I continued to dial the "sick number" but it was busy all day.

739. Call the mental health line and request that they call your employment stating you are ill.

740. While soaking in hot tub, had a stroke and can't move.

741. Take the day off as a result of recent shooting at your worksite.

742. I was accused of child molestation.

743. I went to work and the company re-located to another city, state, and town.

744. I don't have all the necessary training, supplies, etc. to do (perform) my job.

745. Refer to and old calendar (2006) relative to keeping up with work week. Play dumb-you thought it was a holiday.

746. My mother forgot to wake me.

747. I have the Avian Flu.

748. Walk into work smelling like you lived in a gas/smoke tank. State that you came across this cloud while walking to work . . . . now you feel faint.

749. Sign up for Appellate court every Friday for 20 weeks. Most of the time, court will end early and you will have a longer weekend. This works really well if you start court in April.

750. I was car jacked, hijacked or just jacked.

751. I'm held hostage by a fallen power line.

752. I was notified by the Army that my husband, child, significant other was MIA, POW is coming home.

753. I was locked in the back of my trunk for three (3) days.

754. How many times do I have to tell you that I don't work here?

755. That's was not me who called out sick . . . . that was my twin brother, sister.

756. Fake your death.

757. Say that you had jury duty. Check in at the courthouse and leave.

758. Look in the obituary section of the paper on the day you wish to take off. Pretend you know the deceased. You insist that you must attend the funeral. Make sure you get a copy of the obituary to show that you did attend funeral.

759. Volunteer for an assignment nobody wants. Complete the assignment in advance. Get sick. You look good in the boss's eye. No body will ask questions.

760. Eat food one of the co-workers brought in. (this works better if the person cannot cook and the whole office knows this and pretends to eat the persons cooking).

761. Exercise your right to Family Medical Leave.

762. If you have one of those bosses who threatens/or fires you every time something happens, then ½ hour later he hires you back, on that very day he fires you, leave. Tell him that you took him for his word this time.

763. Find hair in your food at a restaurant while out on a working lunch. Choke, get sick, etc. Take the next day off.

764. Call-in and say that someone did a drive-by near your home and you are afraid to go outside.

765. I was hypnotized "not to work".

766. I attended the "Big" parade and a balloon fell on me.

767. Work with glue, paint, or thinner. Faint on the spot.

768. Rant, rave and argue with a sign post . . . . should I say more?

769. Go fishing and take a picture of your big catch. Brag and show off your picture to everyone. The problem is that you don't realize that your "worm" is hanging from your shorts when you took the picture. Are you embarrassed yet?

770. Go to work. Wear a hood over your face/head all day. Say that you are hiding from aliens.

771. Fake your kidnapping.

772. It's just "day work" . . . day work!

773. It's piecework. I made a piece and left.

774. Become a Union Boss or Shop Steward.

775. Just Lie!

776. My middle finger (most productive part of my body) is broken.

777. My boss "George" change my tour . . . I'm calling-in **George**.

778. Fall out the chair at work . . . make sure somebody hears or see you fall.

779. A sinkhole swallowed my car and me.

780. Go out to lunch with your colleagues. Order hot sauce (pretend to get some in your eye)

781. Sabotage the company/business deal the day before . . . . guaranteed you will get plenty of time off.

782. Call-in a bomb threat.

783. Just don't go!

784. Become a complainer. Start complaining about everything-work area, people, coffee, air quality, management style, leadership, company policy, etc. No one will question when you call-out the next day. (They actually will be happy)

785. On the 7th day "He" rested . . . . why not me!?

786. I'm too drunk to drive, fly, talk, walk, etc.

787. You witnessed an accident at work that has left you emotionally unsettled.

788. I just got paid. You expect me to work the day after pay day?

789. I lost my prosthetics (leg, arm hand, nose, etc.).

790. Bomb discovered in my mailbox.

791. Someone duct taped me to the bed. (smile)

792. Memory loss. What day is today?

793. Create an environment were people/co-worked hate being in your presence. (They will encourage you to take off.)

794. Everybody on strike.

795. I was locked in a Port-a-potty all night.

796. I have the Bird Flu disease.

797. I have nothing to wear.

798. Gas too high. Can't afford to drive to work or catch a bus.

799. Driving to work alone is killing me.

800. My wife has athletes' feet.

801. My child was kidnapped right in front of me.

802. My mom fell and broke her hip. I'm seeking medical assistance for her.
Mom fell 2nd time
Mom fell 3rd time
Mom fell 4th time

803. My mom is missing. She has Parkinson disease.

804. I'm taking advantage of "reasonable accommodations" offered by (name the company).

805. The dog ate my keys.

806. I'm on my way to the moon.

807. I'm calling-out by example.

808. There is a Sniper in our area. We were advised by Authorities to stay inside.

809. I'm bored at work. I'm going home tired.

810. I'm feeling Postal.

811. I elect to work from home today.

812. Went to visit gravesite. Left car running without applying emergency brake and it ran over me.

813. At my kid's baseball game, I had a shouting match with the umpire. I did not know that it was "my boss" that was umpiring.

814. Bending over into vehicle to talk with friend, dog walks up behind me and bites me on my ass.

815. There was a shooting at my son/daughters college. The school, police and media are not releasing names of the injured or killed.

816. Stock market crashed.

817. Drink while in uniform. Somebody will make you go home.

818. I witness some illegal work activity. Now I am in hiding.

819. Packed a bag, jumped in a taxi cab and pray that it would take you far away from here.

820. I'm weathering the storm.

821. I'm content sitting at home.

822. I was kidnapped, locked in a trunk and drove into a river left to die.

823. I was left for dead.

824. Went to a party, had a drink and woke up in _____.
    City, state, location

825. It's summertime!

826. Kicked in the head by a mule.

827. I have no place to live.

828. I didn't use a parachute.

829. Take a day off to "get attention".

830. My favorite President died.

831. I'm taking a ME—DAY!

832. The radio DJ told me to take the day off.

833. I am being indicted.

834. I have the "C" word. (Never say what the word is. Let people speculate)

835. I was misdiagnosed.

836. Get a job as an elementary school bus driver. (elementary school bus drivers are always in demand), After your first day, quit . . . . believe it or not, they will be begging you to come back to work (at your convenience of course)

837. A customer spit in my face!

838. I am going to audition to become Americas Next Idol.

839. Someone stole my baby.

840. Ambulance ran into me.

841. I discovered a dead body.

842. Hit in the head with a golf club.

843. Some jerk ran me off the road on my motorcycle.

844. I'm trapped in a train. Stuck in a tunnel beneath the Hudson River.

845. It's raining cats and dogs!?

846. The competitor offered me a job. They will double my salary. I need time to consider option.

847. Snake bite.

848. I was accosted in the company elevator.

849. Immigrants Striking.

850. I found a baby at my doorstep.

851. This is the only way I can take a legitimate vacation without my job calling me, paging me, etc.

852. I love taking a day off.

853. _____ is becoming a habit.
(fill in the blank)

854. Tell your co-workers that you will be late to work the next day. But, you never show up.

855. I'm calling out sick. Working at home.

856. Tsunami/Katrina victims (relative) just move into my home.

857. The robot or computer will do my job white I am not there.

858. Burnt out!

859. My workstation is down (computer).

860. Your husband takes your keys out of your pocketbook (of course you don't know this) he leaves his set of keys in the bedroom; you lock your bedroom door thinking you have your keys . . . . guess what? You don't. You locked yourself out of the house and the bedroom.

861. Your boss takes vacation. You call-out the 1st day he takes his leave and the last day he is due to return.

862. Show signs of breathing problems. You forgot your inhaler. Tell your boss you must go home to get it. Of course when you get home things get worse so you stay home.

863. The Governor shut down the state due to weather, emergency, etc. All non-essential workers are instructed to stay home.

864. I left the top off of the paint thinner. State that you awaken two days later

865. Your working environment has transition from an English-speaking department to a non-English speaking culture. You don't know if co-workers are talking to you, at you or about you.

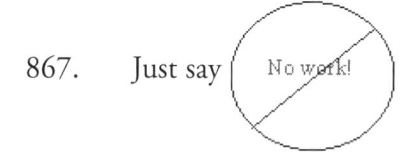

866. With all of the outsourcing implemented . . . I still have a job?

867. Just say ⊘ No work!

868. I am intimidated by all of the little people I work with.

869. I went on a hot air balloon ride and it kept going, going, going, going, going, going (you get the point).

870. While kayaking up the _____ river, we got lost for days.
(fill in the blank)

871. Amnesia.

872. Spider bite. I had an allergic reaction.

873. Bed mites attacked me while I slept.

874. Accumulate one (1) years worth of sick leave. Take the year off using a medical excuse before you officially retire.

875. Always, I mean always get hurt "on the job".

876. Accumulate wealth.

877. I couldn't, wouldn't get up in the morning.

878. It's a blackout and I don't want to leave my wife and children home alone in the dark.

879. My obnoxious co-worker returned to work today.

880. I need the day to make myself beautiful.

881. I had all of my teeth pulled.

882. Kidney failure.

883. I'm stuck at the airport. There was a terrorist attack.

884. Major department store had a "one day sale".

885. As a news writer, I have been charged with espionage in a foreign country.

886. I was shot at the "mall. Police seeking witness.

887. I am a "detainee" at a military base.

888. I came to work to do my job. Got there and somebody else was doing it.

889. Walked into a door and broke my nose (I am a public figure).

890. I was ironing and the cell phone rang, I put the iron to my ear/face by mistake thinking it was the cell phone.

891. The *office party* . . . . (need I say more).

892. Spread of infectious disease.

893. Lingering health problems.

894. Accidentally hit a kid while driving a school bus.

895. My husband/wife/significant other owns the company.

896. I gave birth to my second child today and my 1st child had a heart attack and died. I am experiencing life and death.

897. I've been re-assigned to a new office, building, location.

898. Emotional brain washed by parents that I never had to work.

899. I have been labeled—unproductive.

900. Walking in employee parking lot, the security gate open and closed on my head.

901. The job is taking away too much of "my sense of self"

902. I am feeling unfulfilled. Seeking change.

903. Having a conflict of values, personality or both.

904. I checked my email and I realize I was fired over three weeks ago.

905. The coffee machine is broken.

906. Our computers are down and we have to do everything manually.

907. Have your spouse (significant other) call and say that he/she found you dead. More information to follow.

908. I fell through a hole in the top of my roof. I'm stuck!

909. Went to Vegas on convention. Lost my mind, money and job!?

910. Allergic reaction to peanuts (nuts).

911. I circle the block/lot for several hours. There are "no" parking spots available.

912. I super glued my butt to the toilet . . . . don't ask how!

913. Super Bowl Sunday!

914. While using an electric hammer, I accidentally nailed my finger to the wall.

915. Notify your job 5 days in advance that you will be sick.

916. A plane flew into my building.

917. My job is toxic—there have been reported cases to OSHA.

918. Every time I go to work I get sick.

919. I work around the wrong kind of people!??

920. The job is never ending . . . .

921. I found a dead person in the trunk of my car.

922. Someone set my house on fire . . . . with me in it!

923. Someone through hazardous chemicals in my face as I was walking down the street.

924. Dislocated toe. I cannot wear shoe.

925. Prostaglandin's are being made in my body.

926. My boyfriend told me my vagina could make me a lot of money. I am taking the day off to consider my options.

927. I want/need to soar like an eagle, but I work with a bunch of turkeys who are holding me back.

928. Get a job where the "boss" hates his job as much as you do. He/she will understand when you need a day off.

929. Send your twin to replace you at work.

930. I work with a group of haters.

931. Get a flu shot offered by your job. Verbally state that the shot has made you sick.

932. Have your computer call you out sick.

933. Your church organization is selling fish dinners. You take fish orders from all of your co-workers on Wednesday. Thursday, you call

out sick. Friday you delivery fish order to co-workers. Everybody understands why you took the day off. (to clean fish of course)

934. I'm living up to your stereotype that I am lazy and don't want to work.

935. My boss told me to take a "sick day". He was sick of me.

936. It's a "New Years" resolution to take a day off.

937. Working with (insert name) today jeopardizes my future employment opportunities.

938. I need a day to "break out of the limiting roles that box me in"

939. I need to free myself from emotional traps at work.

940. I'm fed up and frustrated with a colleague whose incompetence is driving me crazy.

941. I'm escaping a boss who gets angry because I am not a mind reader.

942. I'm detaching from annoying co-workers whose irritating habits ruin my day.

943. I'm protecting my personal and professional space from boundary busters.

944. I have been transported back in time where Kings and Queens do not work.

945. Let the robot prove it can replace me.

946. I do not work with "like minded people". Why spend time with people who aren't similar?

947. Kiss the "ring" or die!

948. Kiss the ground, shoe, spouse, that your boss walks on.

949. The public service announcement states "if you are coughing, sneezing, running a fever, ... stay home".

950. I follow the lead. If the boss is out, I'm out!

951. I fake it all the time with my husband but I can't fake working 9 to 5.

952. The boss doesn't want me to come to work sick, but he doesn't trust that I am ill.

953. The company business went bankrupt.

954. It's below zero degrees outside and your office temperature is reading minus 12.

955. In the pursuit of happiness, joy and peace.

956. I'm being phased out of my job, business etc.

957. I am having dinner with the Queen.

958. I have tickets to the Oprah Winfrey show!

959. Look out the window—we have 102 inches of snow.

960. It's Tax day—April 15th. I'm getting my taxes prepared.

961. Steroid user!

962. I'm at the (ass doctor). No need to ask questions, use your imagination.

963. I have fallen head-first into a narrow water meter enclosure while working in my yard.

964. My 16 year old has "mono" and I suspect my 13 years old has it also. It is contagious.

965. The stock market crashed! The number kept going down, down, down . . . .

966. Day off recipe
Ingredients:
Job, time, boredom, sick, unappreciated, moody boss, dumb ass co-workers, low wages, fed up

Mix:
Job, time, boredom and unappreciated until well blended. (Blending time may vary depending on attitude and longevity on the job. Gradually add moody boss, dumb ass co-workers. Top with low wages.

Temperature
Fed-up should be set at simmering. Anything higher will result in total burn out.

Enjoy your day off.

967. I will always be guided to do and say the things that contribute to my well being. I quit!

968. Rule #1
"If you don't take care of the employee, somebody else will"

969. Retirement is too far away. I'm leaving now!

970. Relieve Stress . . . . take a day off!

971. Cuss out your boss and tell him/her how incompetent he really is.

972. You spread a rumor that you are going to need time off for something major . . . never state what the major is . . . let the rumor mill decide.

973. Call your information help-desk regarding a computer problem. The help desk instructs you to remove wires, plug in prompts, and

remove stuff from under your desk. As you do all of this, something electrical sparks and you scream. Go home.

974. Who? What? Where? When? Why? How? (RIGHT NOW!)

975. I did not get the promotion.

976. I just got promoted and I was instructed to take some time off to absorb the good news.

977. Stranded at the airport, runway, etc.

978. I work with kids all day. (You're guaranteed to catch something)

979. I was assaulted while trying to teach.

980. Have you ever eaten my wife's cooking!?

981. My fellow sanitation-engineering friend was fatally injured on the job.

982. My therapist is out of town and I must find her.

983. Wear a T-shirt that says: "Kill the boss day".

984. As a farmer, the sun never rose, the rooster did not crow and the crops never grew.

985. Start to "ssssss . . . . t.t.t.t t t t t t t t t t t.t uuuuuuuu . . . . tttttttttt . . . er at work. Do this every time you open your mouth. No one will question why you took the next day off.

986. We forgot to get the Sunday paper off the porch, and when we found it the next day (Monday). We thought it was Sunday.

987. I had ~~diahre dyrea direathe~~ the shits.

988. Lance a pimple while at work using a paper clip . . . . the next day report that you suspect infection.

989. Accused of fraudulent work ethics. Take the time off to allow employer to re-consider options that are in your favor.

990. I was humiliated on national TV.

991. The preacher "flogged" me in front of the congregation on Sunday.

992. Received letter from Bone Marrow Donor registry. They need me to report today.

993. You work in an office full of menopausal-middle age women. One minute it's too hot, the next it's cold or everyone is feeling suicidal. (This is enough to go insane)

994. The DJ stated racist remarks on the air about me as a person. I am boycotting!

995. Call-in on April 1st and state that you quit! Return to work the next day and say "April Fool'!

996. Embezzle money from the company using your boss computer access, log-on ID.

997. My horoscope/numerology predicted that this was not a good day for working.

998. There are no jobs in the United States. Everything is Global.

999. Timing is everything! Wait for the right situation, time of day, location, and people to work with, boss and need.

1000. You are a radio Deejay. Open your mouth and state something racially offensive on the air.

1001. Write a book and become wealthy enough to retire from your job.

Printed in Great Britain
by Amazon